STRANGER ON THE PLANET

*The Small
Book of Laurie*

STRANGER ON THE PLANET

The Small
Book of Laurie

CLAIRE BURCH

REGENT PRESS
1997

Library of Congress Cataloging-in-Publication Data

Burch, Claire
     Stranger on the planet : the small book of Laurie / Claire Burch.
        p.   cm.
     ISBN 0-916147-67-3 (pbk.)
     1. Dually diagnosed persons--United States--Biography. 2. Dually
diagnosed persons--Care--United States. I. Title.
RC564.68.B87 1997
616.89'0092--dc21
[B]
                                   96-49077
                                     CIP

Manufactured in the United States of America
REGENT PRESS
6020-A Adeline
Oakland, CA 94608

"There is a three word solution to the crisis. Housing, housing, housing"

—*Robert Hayes, Founder,* Coalition for the Homeless

"The homeless are simply surplus souls in a system firmly rooted in competition and self interest, in which only the strongest (ie; those who fit most snugly within the confines of a purely arbitrary norm) will survive."

—*Mitch Snyder, Homeless Advocate*

Foreword

WHEN I WOKE UP THIS MORNING I had a day-
dream so strong it filled the room with
beauty. Laurie wasn't in pain because of a defective
gene and an infancy so abandoned that her fright and
suspicion at five months, which was when I took her
to raise, was already so dug in that it never completely went away. This morning she was a singing, laugh-
ing, joyful child with a twinkle in her eye and a
sweetness everyone couldn't help noticing.

So I stretched out my arms and she said, "Mom,
you came for me," and we were back in the green
skunk-cabbage filled meadow next to Long Pond and
we were trying to attract the attention of the biggest
bull frog as we had done so long ago.

When somebody dies it is so sad, even if it means
you'll have more time for your own work and play,
and won't have to be on the phone most of the time,
hunting for a place where she could live, a place or
person who could help.

What help there was, was scant. Some of it came
from people like Cris, the last patient's advocate she
ever did see, and the first to take her side and help

me get her out of the locked unit where she had gone down so fast, as I knew she would, even though she had been desperate enough this time to sign herself in while I was away. Truth to tell, we all failed her. I was so often angry at her and so sorry now that I was not as kind to her about her failings as I usually am to other people about their failings. That's what I most regret.

Regrets however, are not what is needed now.

What is needed is a clear logical look at the economics of housing people who have never been able to take care of themselves but who are still human beings who have committed no crime and need a decent affordable place to stay.

Landlords won't rent to people whose credit ratings are pages long with unpaid hospital bills, even if their moms are willing to pay security and first and last.

The Lanterman Petris Short bill gave patients the right to "just say no" to psychotropics that can sometimes cause tardive dyskinesia (an incurable movement disorder).

A bill needs to exist that can put a roof over the heads of those doomed to wander from single room hotel to motel to furnished room to street to shelter forever because they can't keep it together for reasons of the mind.

Laurie died eight days ago. I actually tasted a gift of lemon cake tonight and so said my first goodbye to her. Angels, please keep this child safe.

Forgive us, the living, for not having been able to help you to a life of your own. Forgive us for not finding the means to allay the anxiety that pushed you towards booze or too many pills every day of your life after you grew up. Nobody knew how reluctant you were to put your feet down from the bed in the morning, so afraid the world would fall away.

Forgive me for failing you at the end, for listening to authorities again. For not taking you for a walk in the woods when you told me you'd left the detox. The last day I had worked until seven, editing a book for a doctor who was going away for two months and needed the first draft to be finished.

We were going to spend the next day together, looking for a new place. When I took you from the hospital the day before, I had wanted to find a cottage by a river with a lot of tall grass in front. Maybe there would have been a puppy there of no particular breed, with affectionate eyes.

We could have walked to town for pizza and caught a movie and finished up with strawberry ice cream. And I would have been grateful to be "codependent" again and you would still have been alive.

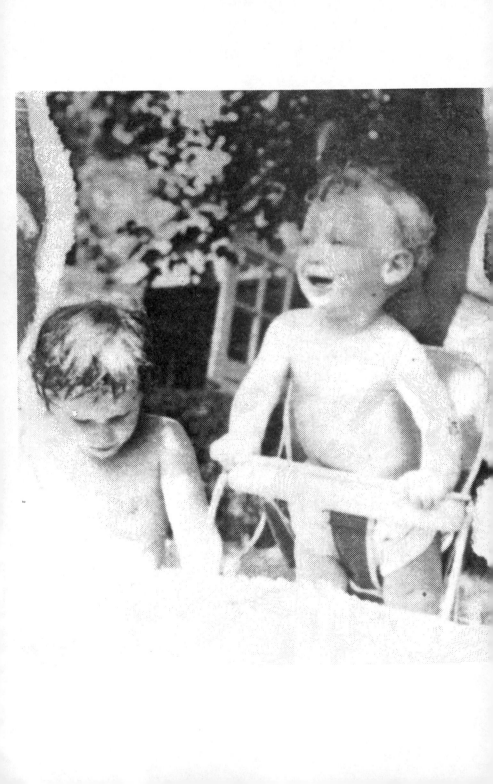

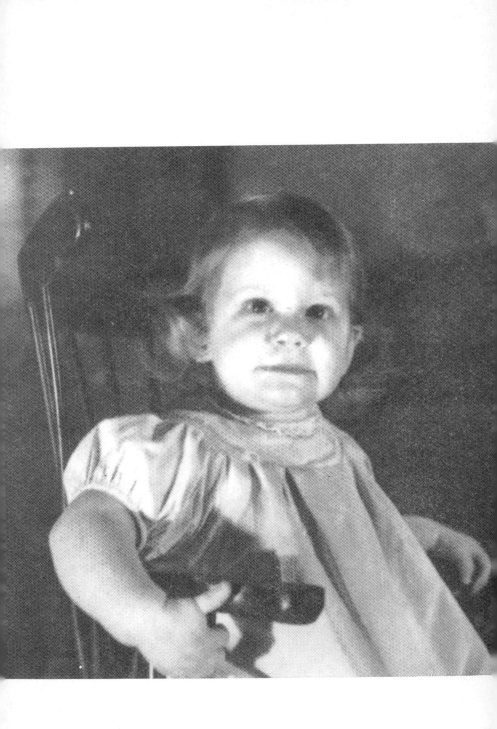

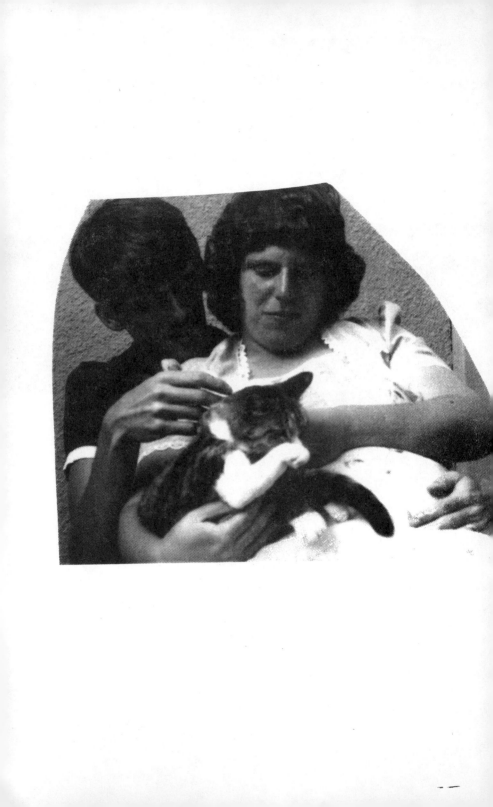

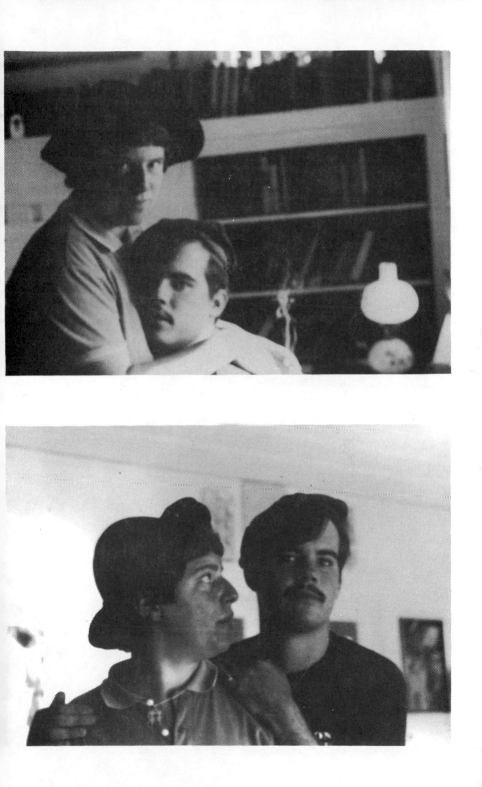

Drawings &
Paintings
by Laurie

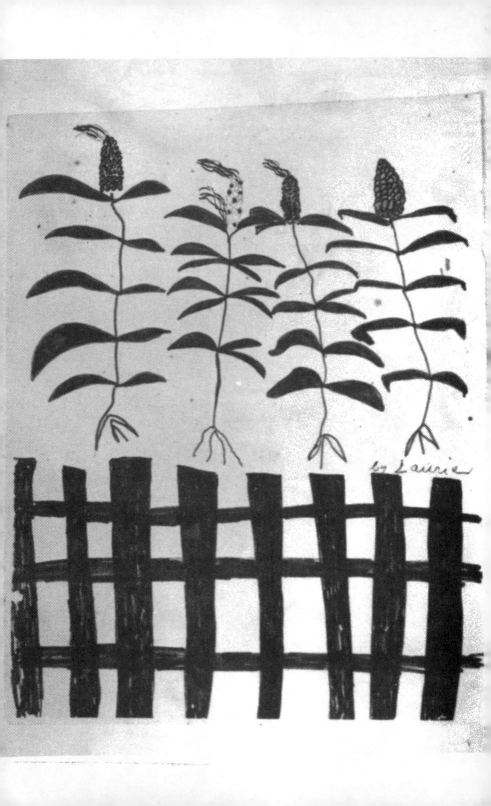

Laurie Bure

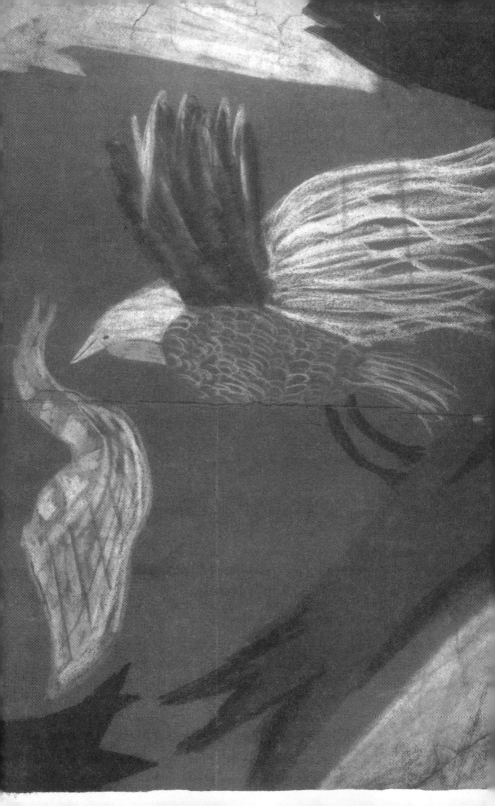

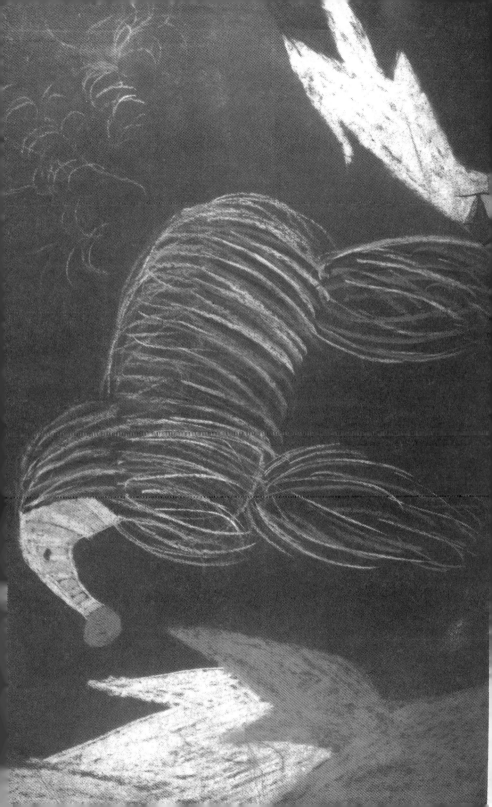

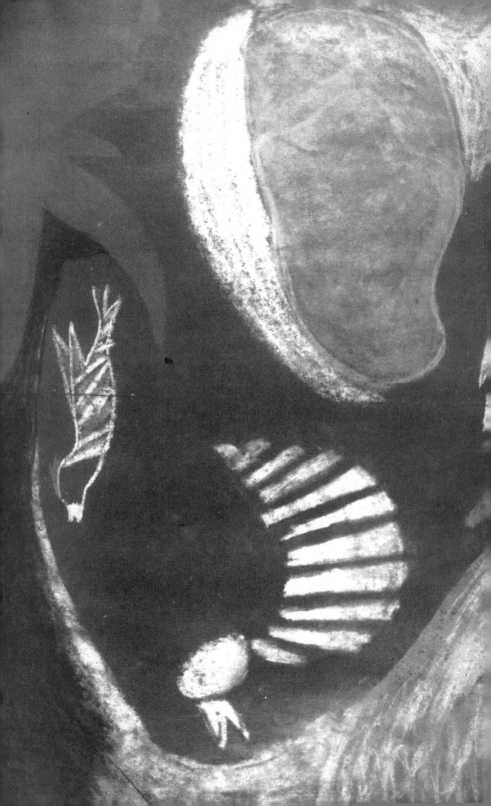

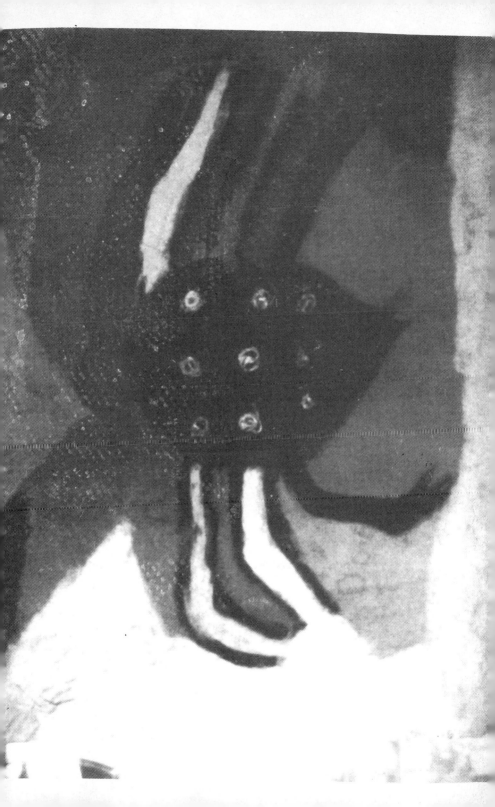

Laurie, blood-stained,
after having been beaten
up by her drunk
boyfriend. Her favorite
picture—God, guiding a
boy at the helm,
is behind her

Could It Have Been Different?

LAURIE WAS SCARED as a baby and she stayed scared all her life no matter how hard I tried to make her safe. Often, as she'd get up in the morning, she'd put her feet tentatively over the side of the bed, afraid the floor wouldn't be there.

Laurie was one of many many thousands who had been given the label of "Dual Diagnosis," mental illness and chemical dependency. Nutty laws regarding medical insurance for the disabled are still the rule in most states.

Each year their hospitalizations (frequent) cost families or the government well over a hundred thousand dollars each. For a tiny portion of that amount, Laurie and others like her, hooked on anxiety long before substances, could have received all year help in decent cottage model halfway houses.

Since the Reagan years, many of the halfway houses or residential community mental health centers have closed. Most of the others have waiting lists up to several years. People like Laurie go from emergency to emergency and cannot wait for the long periods necessary. Most of the board and care homes are unspeakable.

Closing the large state hospitals made sense. Understaffing and overuse of psychotropics often caused the irreversible movement disorder known as tardive dyskinesia. But the great community mental health residential centers that were to replace these hospitals never happened.

I AM TELLING ABOUT Laurie's life for a reason. There are others out there who still desperately need what she needed. I loved her, tried to help, and ultimately failed. I don't know where the blame lies. Her birth mother was never able to function on her own, and had to give her up at a month. I finally located her birth family when she was grown. I had this wishful-thinking storybook idea that maybe we could share responsibility for her, since her problems and pain were so intense. It made it real hard for the children born to me after Laurie was adopted.

That fairytale expectation quickly ended as I discovered the helplessness of her birth mother and the pattern of addiction and dependency that ran through that extended family. Laurie had not been the only baby given up for adoption nor her birth mother the only one on long term psychotropics. I was told that her birth father had been an alcoholic who vanished into the wild blue yonder.

The controversy about nature versus nurture, genetic inheritance versus climate of upbringing, continues to this day. Though theories of causation have changed and parent bashing is no longer as frequent or as fashionable as in the Fifties, stigmatizing diagnoses are still given out like candy by some label obsessed "authorities". They gave her one when she was a small "wild child."

The label given when Laurie was not yet three, was child schizophrenia. The near destruction of our family stemmed straight from too free a use of that word and the terror it started. This was the time frame when parents were blamed for all pathology. If a child had a problem, even respectable and indeed brilliant mind explorers like Laing and Estersen suggested in such books as *Families of Schizophrenics* that a malignant pall lay over the household, consisting of screwed up interpersonal communications like double-binds, mystification etc. This was often the case, but in truth it was a "Why does a chicken cross the road? To get to the other side....Which came first, the chicken or the egg?" kind of situation in which it was, and still is, impossible to tell what preceded what, and what was reactive to what. The Margaret Mahler theory of unconscious rejection in infancy causing bizarre behavior became a self-fulfilling prophecy as helpless folk like us, thinking "but we loved this child," wondered what our unconscious was doing to make trouble.

If it's unconscious, you can't, by definition, know. Right? After a while we were all crazy.

Laurie is Gone

LAURIE IS GONE. They are doing an autopsy this afternoon. She was found in a room at the Motel 6 in Walnut Creek. She had barred her door from the inside. I kept calling there all last night and this morning. I told them I was worried. I asked them to send someone in to check on her. They said they would do it after checkout time. Finally they said the door was barred from the inside. They called the police to break down the door. April is the cruelest month. Even TS Eliot knew it before it happened. She must have gotten pills somewhere.

Laurie died April 14, 1994. She was found on the floor of a room she had rented the night before. She had taken too much of something and she left no note.

I had come back from a trip to New York to see my mother on April 11. The next morning I went to the hospital where Laurie was in a locked unit. She had signed herself in a few days before because she knew she needed help. She hated locked units with a vengeance but she didn't have a choice. She had used up her medical insurance days for chemical dependency in an open unit.

She signed herself in on April 6, her father's birthday. He had died when she was fifteen and she had never gotten over his death. They put her in seclusion and restraints when they found her needles. It made her worse. Much worse.

She had drowned her pain with alcohol for twenty years and when her body could no longer take it, she turned to pills. Someone gave her heroin and it must have been another thing to help the pain go away. She died like Lenny Bruce, perhaps for some of the same reasons.

We adopted her when she was five months old. She had been abandoned to the Department of Welfare at one month, and placed in a foster home. It was a very bad foster home. It was what they called a "baby farm" and the woman lost her license shortly after we took her home.

She was a beautiful baby but the hardest one I ever raised. It took all my strength to briefly make her happy. Nothing made her happy for long; her bottle was too cold or too hot, the world too unfriendly, her skin too thin.

She was jealous of her brother and sisters as they came after her and through me instead of an adoption agency. She was five when her brother died at a year and a half, and I tried to continue to take good care of her. I was a pretend alive person for a long time after that and she was smart enough to know it. She was sensitive enough to feel it. My strength began to return when the other two girls were born, but hers never did.

We took her to shrinks and they gave her serious

psychiatric names, as she wasn't able to face regular life like the other children. The diagnoses followed her and became repeated from doctor to doctor, hospital to hospital, until I learned to conceal them, and present her as she presented herself, a substance abuser, which had more prestige in this society. Much of my life has been spent trying to beat the rap of her diagnoses. Most of her life went down the tubes trying to do the same.

She had been a beautiful teenager and was still beautiful when I took her from the hospital on Tuesday and brought her to an addiction center two towns over. She had begun to lose some of the weight she had gained when she began to use food as solace after breaking up with the person she loved and had been with for five years. He was a heavy alcoholic; their relationship was stormy.

She wanted to go to Portland and make a fresh start, but she was too ill and in too much pain to get it together.

She didn't like it at the Center. There were rough people there and she was scared. She called me the next day and said she had left with a friend and gone to the Motel 6. I was working yesterday and said I would see her today.

She called and told me her friend had been discharged from the hospital and taken a room at the motel. He was going to drive her here the next morning and we were going to help her get into a clean and sober house where she would have a support system and her own room. And she could cook there—she liked to cook.

At eleven she called me and said she was in a lot of pain and couldn't stay with him, even as a friend. She needed a space of her own. He helped her with money for another room in the same place. I worried and wondered about her asking him because I knew she had enough money left to get it herself.

She must have used the extra money to get heroin. Somebody said she had gone to Chinatown in San Francisco to get it.

I called the motel five times during the night because she had said she'd call me back and I knew how depressed she was. He kept calling her room too. The clerk kept telling us she had gone out. I called all morning because I had a feeling something was wrong. I figured she would call me by checkout time because she'd be needing some financial help. When she hadn't answered her phone at twelve noon I asked them to send someone to her room. They said she had latched it from the inside and called the police who broke down the door.

They found Laurie on the floor and she was gone.

I have some accusations to make. I do not accuse any *person* of helping hasten my daughter's death. I accuse the system, the system that is responsible for making care for people with emotional problems and chemical dependency problems, a low priority in the annual budget of this country.

People like my daughter, who were always given what is called a dual diagnosis, are strangers on this planet. You see them wander by, often in some dire emergency, usually in pain of one kind or another. They live in a thousand places, go to hospitals for a few days take a geographical escape often, hoping that a new place will make things better.

They need more help than they get, and they need it now.

How and When the Dream Began

THIS IS THE STORY OF LAURIE. She was born to an unwed mother on Staten Island, New York before it was fashionable to be a single parent. Abandoned to the Department of Welfare at a month, she was placed into a foster home that later lost its license (the infants had all been neglected).

At five months she was adopted by us. When she was four, her brother Tommy was born to us. He died when she was five and a half.

When she was six, her sister Emily was born.

Her sister Elizabeth was born when she was nine.

When Laurie started school, she changed her name from Robin to Laura, no one knew why. She always had problems getting along, and finally had to be tutored at home and then needed a special school. My husband had died when she was sixteen and her sisters were little.

She was a hard child to raise and was given a serious psychiatric diagnosis at a very early age.

That diagnosis was to follow her from "authority" to "authority" until finally I learned to conceal it when taking her for the help she needed frequently.

After her father's death she turned to hard drugs and alcohol and for the rest of her life she was told that she had what is called a "dual diagnosis."

She preferred to think of herself as a substance abuser because when she had been sent to the adolescent unit after a suicide attempt following her father's death, she felt stigmatized and abused.

Doctors had told us to institutionalize her, as continuing to raise her would be too hard on the other children. We had not been able to accept this advice.

Observing how she had deteriorated in the adolescent unit of NY Psychiatric Institute, I was not able to give up. After my husband's death I tried as hard as I could to keep the children apart. At first I took the doctors' advice and hospitalized Laurie again. Again she got worse there so I knew that she needed to be free, despite her problems.

This meant that Laurie had a life. Although her freedom meant that she encountered danger, it also let her taste the joy of relationships, many transitory, two of them deep and often loving.

Her first marriage lasted a weekend, and was annulled.

Her second was to someone she didn't love at all but she was in her born again Christian phase and thought God was telling her to marry him. It lasted two unhappy years. She was sad after that and gave up on Fundamentalism.

Then she met Charles and spent the happiest two years of her life. The marriage was to last seven years but the last part of it was marred by what would happen when she drank (and her drinking had begun again,

STRANGER ON THE PLANET: *The Small Book of Laurie*

escalating and combined with pills, a lot of them).

In this marriage her husband had glimpsed what few had seen in her, a bawdy uninhibited sense of humor, though so often swamped with anxiety. She was childlike in an adult world, lacking the usual persona necessary to make it.

Her other deep relationship occurred a few years after the inevitable divorce and a series of one night stands.

It was with Karl who shared her sense of playfulness but was already lost himself, turned over to the state and a group home at fourteen, a confirmed alcoholic and addict even then, but more so in his twenties.

For almost six years their relationship teetered in a slow dance of blackouts, binges and seizures, punctuated by bouts, blows, trashed apartments and emotional reunions that usually lasted only a few days.

After him she was weary and never had a strong feeling relationship again, only a series of hopeful moments followed by batterings and anguished endings.

She was sinking, and nobody could help. She hadn't heard from him in over a year, but he'd called, unexpectedly, that last week.

After her last conversation with him, a day before she died, she called me. "I spoke with Karl and it's hopeless," she had said. Later he told me she'd asked him for drugs. She had said that his speech was slurred again and she finally knew it would never get better, so had given up. I think she was telling the truth because when he'd asked me for her number earlier his speech had already been slurred. Later I thought I shouldn't have given it to him, but he'd said he still loved her, and I knew she still loved him, despite the heavy problem. So I hadn't wanted to play God.

In later years Laurie's body could no longer take alcohol. She had been in almost constant physical pain since an accident in '79 (her husband had lost control of the car and she'd gone through the windshield onto the highway). It was a rented car; he'd failed to get insurance and told the police it was his fault, so there was no compensation. After that she'd begun to take huge quantities of prescription painkillers. Doctors were unaware that she went to other doctors with the same requests. Her need had become out of control.

She tried many "geographical escapes." All of them failed. When she was away she would call me as often as six or eight times a day, frightened and lonely.

AA and NA became her life. Her friends were always people she met at meetings, her needs so engulfing that they usually turned away after a while.

She was ripped off and beaten up regularly, her judgment colored by her longing for company to fill a hollow in her heart.

Her final six years were punctuated by brief voluntary hospitalizations and the love-hate relationship with Karl, who was sometimes caring towards her, but had a heavy drinking and hard drug habit of his own.

I found apartments for her, but she was never able to stay in them alone. Karl trashed many of them, so I stopped coming up with security deposits and signing leases.

In her last year she went for medical detoxes many times. Each of these brief hospitalizations cost the state many thousands of dollars. After five or six days she would be discharged and given a xeroxed list of recovery places. All of them required residents to have medical clearance and be off all mind-altering pills like valium, barbiturates, painkillers.

The hospitals wouldn't give her medical clearance as the number of days her insurance would cover was never enough to get her safely off them.

The dual diagnosis recovery places, which allowed some of the medications she was still on, all had long waiting lists.

Gradually she became another of the thousands of "walking wounded", wandering through a system that never helped her stay anywhere long enough to get over her addictions.

The money that went for her frequent brief hospitalizations could have kept her in a luxurious "retirement home" such as exists for the elderly, at far less annual cost. With a nurse and visiting doctor, people with dual diagnoses, "strangers on the planet" would no longer have to wander, exiles and outsiders in a society that exposes its people on the fringe to the pushers of heroin and crack.

Try as she might, I couldn't help her find a living situation that worked for more than a few days.

People told me to withdraw my help, spouting the new cultural clichés about codependency.

It was when I went away for ten days, because of a family emergency, that someone gave her heroin again.

On her father's birthday, she signed herself into a locked unit, knowing she was hooked.

The found her needles and paraphernalia and put her in seclusion and restraints.

When I came back a week later, the old deterioration had already begun.

She begged me to take her out as a hold had been placed. I was told they would lift the hold if she was taken to a recovery center or a detox.

I took her to a non-medical detox. It was the early part of the month so she still had enough money for a motel if it didn't work out. She left that night. Someone had assaulted her and she was frightened. She went to a motel in Walnut Creek.

A friend was going to drive her back here the next day and we had a new list of "clean and sober" houses she was going to explore. These were called T. L. C. houses.If it didn't work out she was going to try Portland.

She died some time that night, by the needle.

It will take two to eight weeks for the toxicology report.

She left a book of poetry, some drawings, and the indelible image of a curious child, often anxious and insecure, wading along the bank of Long Pond, looking for something she never found. I, who tried to help her find it, for all these years, time after time after time, still wonder what she was looking for, and why it was—and still is—nowhere to be found.

End of the Dream

ONE MORNING IN AUGUST I wake up in tears thinking of all the young men who have died of AIDS, whose poignant obituaries I had read in a newspaper before falling asleep the night before. The taste of salt leads me to the word kosher and the word kosher leads me to say my four lines of Kaddish over and over as the world struggles into daylight.

So of course the next thought is of Laurie.

I go to the next room where three and a half months before I had emptied her bag, her pack and her purse that the coroner's office had returned to me, looking for a clue, a word. There had been none, only the mute spectacle of the following objects, all carefully put back at that time.

I spread them out now on a sofa and look at them once more, knowing it is time to pack them away though perhaps not the questions they provoke. Her purse contains:

A small handbook titled *The Rights of Mental Patients.*

A pack of Winston lights and a half pack of Winston regulars.

Two travellers check receipts.
An April Med-i-Cal card.
A withdrawal slip signed Pat.
A Versatel Card that had expired five years before.
A Patient's Rights Advocate card.
A hospital visitors hours card.
A card on which was scribbled "My mother is
    coming tonight".
A MEDICARE card.
A bottle of phenobarbital.
Another hospital card for a different hospital.
A prescription for Darvon.

On the back of the Darvon prescription is written "$5 for photo, $12 every day, each dose, 2nd and Townsend St. Catch Bart to SF Powell St station. Then catch 30 Stockton bus to Townsend and 4th. Walk to 2nd. Then you're there.

I knew this must have been a methadone clinic and remembered (and so regretted) my response when she told me she'd be going to a methadone program daily.

"Oh no," I'd said, not realizing the alternatives. "I read that methadone is the most addictive of all. You'll be hooked for life and it'll take all your time and all your money." I'd suggested that she go into a hospital detox and get help with the withdrawal instead. She'd listened to me but I'd been wrong; she'd gotten punished instead of helped. To that particular staff, her addiction was a shocking crime deserving seclusion and restraints.

I stare at the rest of the contents of her purse, wondering if anything had been missed that would tell me why her life had ended in such a sad and solitary hurry. There are no new insights as I continue this quick hopeless inventory.

A card that says "Theodore sober-cook-drummer" with a beeper number. A friend from A.A? I call the number. He is shocked, but he had only met her once, at a meeting. He barely remembers her.

A discarded nursing station census form with four names.

On the back she had scribbled these words: "I spoke to Karl today. He sounded drunk of course. I finally give up."

A few pages torn from a Hazelton book that starts "Grandiosity is an exalted state of mind common to the addicted man or woman."

A California picture ID which expired 12/05/93.

Two tortoise shell berets, a cloth ponytail holder, a pink toothbrush and a broken silverplate buckle.

A piece of paper that says "Laurie—address: Anytown USA."

I call my mother to tell her I am coming to visit in a few weeks and ask her opinion about the cemetery stuff.

I tell her I intend to find an engraver who will carve a sentence in Laurie's memory on her father's gravestone. There are no graves left in the cemetery where her father is buried and where half her ashes have been sprinkled. The cemetery won't allow another stone and forbids anything for another person being written on an existing stone. As the plot is filled, except for my sister's, and I can't buy another, four engravers have already turned me down.

She tells me it is impossible, that if the cemetery finds the name of a second person, they will say it breaks their rule and perhaps even remove her father's stone because of the infraction.

I say I intend to make a test case of it.

It infuriates me that there is still no place for her to be admitted and accepted, even in death. Her ashes are sprinkled but not acknowledged.

I resolve to find a maverick engraver somewhere who will take a chance. After all, it's not like painting graffiti on cars in Singapore. I only want them to write her name, her dates, and the words "Angels Keep This Child Safe."

Some people come into this world more sensitive to pain and conflict stimuli than others. Laurie was clearly one of them.

For whatever reason, biological, genetic, environmental, pressures which can be dealt with by some, cause breakdowns in others.

To be grownup in this culture and not cause harm involves keeping our ears open to the problems of people who think and behave differently, however diagnosed or labeled.

These voices of others lead to awareness of people balanced precariously over a chasm, one foot on the top of each mountain.

Those of us who are successful at maintaining this balance are able to keep our authentic inner life and manage the kind of outward reality that somehow satisfies our own needs, as well as the demands of the society in which we live.

When we make judgements without compassion, designating people who cannot balance in this way as "crazy", we banish them, treat them as outsiders, and therefore deprive ourselves of what they can contribute.

We might think of what is known as emotional disturbance as existing in a different state during which perceptions are altered, often temporarily.

We can understand this if we think of the so called "crazy" person as on a drug that makes him or her see and experience things differently sometimes.

How can we help?

A society that banishes its people on the fringe is a stale society. We need to provide safety, protection, and understanding.

We need to let people go through their "numbers" without judgement or rejection, unless they are hurting others or themselves.

Locked units, for people who have committed no crime, are not an answer.

Abandonment to the streets is not an answer.

Answers lie in attitude change, acceptance of "oddness," providing warm, supportive living arrangements that reduce anxiety and guarantee safety.

Answers lie in better, kinder care and walk-in centers without red tape, instantly available when people are experiencing sensations that frighten them.

Nobody, unless violent towards self or others, should be deprived of major life experiences. That these experiences may seem chancy is a judgement that should be discarded, for a happy moment is fixed forever as a happy moment.

Ashes

T<small>HE FIRST TIME</small> I ever thought of ashes was
when Barton Benes, a sculptor at Westbeth
in New York where we lived, brought me a present of
the ashtray made of the ashes of Hans Schneider, a former SS man. Westbeth was a block long, subsidized
artist's project constructed from the old Bell Telephone
building, where the first sound movie was shown, it
being Al Jolsen in "The Jazz Singer." Westbeth had
four hundred apartments.

Barton had a box containing the ashes of Hans
Schneider delivered to him by mistake, and as his
middle name is Lidice, he proceeded to avenge the
small town in Europe, which had been wiped out
during the massacre of World War Two when Nazi
soldiers killed everyone, by making ashtrays out of
his ashes. As I was his and Howard's dear friend, he
gave me the first one, marked but unsigned.

I still have the ashtray but experience it as
spooky and Jane had said Yume wanted his ashes to
be mixed with his wife's and sprinkled, and rumor
had it that Yume's wife's ashes were still in a brown
paper bag in Jim Moore's apartment since Jim had let

him stay there until he was so sick that I had hunted up his Medicare number and got him into Alta Bates, where he lay, washed daily and on clean sheets, until he died.

Much later, after everyone had paid their respects except Ace who announced that Yume had been a pervert and was quickly jumped by the others, we all realized that we were never going to get it together to redeem Yume's ashes. Ben Felsher said, "Lost and gone forever, gone forever, Clementine" and flung his arms out in a Hippie Buddhist kind of gesture of defeat.

So when I was told that my third daughter was dead, had died of an overdose, I had already been introduced to the idea of ashes.

I wanted to bury her back East, where we had been from, and I wanted her to have a funeral like her father had had, dignified and impressive, not exactly John Kennedy in a flag covered caisson drawn by prancing white horses, but not just lost in the system somewhere, like what had happened to Yume's ashes.

But she couldn't be buried back east where her father was, with a stone like his and some gentle inscription, because the situation was this: the family plot had held room for five graves originally. In a weak moment, during my last year in high school, my parents had let one of the graves be taken by my best friend's mother, as my best friend, age seventeen, was alone in the world when her mother died and didn't know where she could put her mother.

Through the years two more of the five plots had

STRANGER ON THE PLANET: *The Small Book of Laurie*

been used, one for my son Thomas who had died at a year and a half, and one for my husband who had never got over that or the time during the war when his best friend Guff had stepped on a mine and had his legs blown off and my husband had picked him up and tried to carry him to where he could put on tourniquets but there had been a burst of mortar fire and my husband dropped him. Then he had picked him up again and then there had been another burst of mortar fire, so he had dropped him and run and didn't look back this time and of course he never saw him again and had never forgiven himself.

So then the next grave was used for my father. There had been a regular rabbi there who had whispered to me that if I wanted he'd say an extra prayer for the baby since he'd noticed Tommy's grave next to where we were about to put the coffin, so of course I said yes, not yet being a believer but thinking to hedge my disbelief in case, and I found out later he'd billed my sister who'd been given the check to be in charge of the arrangements, an extra fifty bucks for his prayer.

What that left in the way of graves in the family plot was two, and of course one of them was going to have to be for my mom so she could be next to daddy.

So when the subject came up I'd said my sister could have the last one as I understand that all through childhood she did more of the dishes than I did and babysat our kid brother more, and had worked in the store at the cosmetics counter after school without pay while I only delivered prescriptions and had managed to get out of putting in regular hours.

That was why the only way anybody else was going to get in there would have to be by way of ashes being sprinkled, unless we were going to be layered, something I don't think the cemetery rules would have allowed.

As there was therefore no place to bury my daughter, I decided I would have her cremated. This would probably work out as I'd some time ago decided to get myself cremated as well when I die, for the same reason, the family plot would be full, except for my sister's space, so the only way I could sneak back in would be to be sprinkled.

Regarding myself I figured I could clarify my wishes to Mark, my longtime companion. They are that half of me should be sprinkled where he thinks he'll eventually land, as I have loved and been with him for over twenty years now and hope eventually to make fertilizer with him. Wait, that sounds weird. I intend to precede him in the magic journey by many years and would not be in any hurry, or troubled that my ashes be alone for some time.

Well, all these are not terribly cheery thoughts but they did pass though my mind as we were going through the red tape of securing my daughter's ashes.

As the toxicology report can take up to eight weeks, I still don't know exactly what happened but I do know that we took her ashes back in a copper looking box and that before mailing it to my brother and sister-in-law overnight express registered, to be sprinkled around her father's grave, I pried open the box to bury some of her ashes in the little garden I was planting for her around the side where the big garbage can sits, though when I find the key to the gate I plan to move it inside the fence out of view despite that Mark or I would have to bring it down to the sidewalk every Tuesday since that's collection day.

Actually I tried to pry open the box for almost an hour, in the process breaking a Phillips and a regular screwdriver and the crocodile brass paper cutter that had belonged to her father. As I didn't succeed in prying it open though I had three sides almost there, I waited until Mark came home and he finished the job.

I cried when I buried the cupful of ashes I had scooped out with my best china cream pitcher and never will use again for anything but tiny souvenirs left, like her ponytail holders and barrettes, her reading glasses and the last of her last package of Winston lights.

I forgot that her ashes came a day after her memorial which we held Monday evening. It was like her to be a day late for the occasion, but, like many of the times she'd been late before, it wasn't only her fault but also the society, the nation, the inequity of medical insurance benefits, and the harsh genetic hand she had been dealt, that partly determined her inability to show up anywhere on time that became one of the factors in her always having been given what is called a dual diagnosis, schizophrenia and chemical dependency.

Had she been Marilyn Monroe they would have had her toxicology report in a couple of days. Her ashes would have been available by the early edition the following morning and other signs of belated respect would have been paid.

At any rate when I sprinkled what was left of the cup I said as much of Kaddish as I could. The day before, Mark's sister's husband Levy who was a rabbi had kindly faxed a phonetic version from Israel. I had tried to read it aloud the way it looked, but unfortunately it was a Sephardic version and the pronunciation I had learned from Mark's friend, Mark Elber, was the Ashkenazi version and try as I might I couldn't unlearn it.

Nevertheless it looked beautiful in Hebrew but when I went and read it in English I was sorely disappointed and even pissed because it seemed to take no notice of the person I was grieving over, only kept repeating these assorted loyalty oaths to Lord God King of the Universe, which I actually perceived as somewhat self indulgent (on the part of God I mean).

Not being able to think of another prayer I continued to repeat the first three lines of the Ashkenazi version, repressing my indignation as to how the prayer seemed to actually ignore my hurt and heartbroken daughter and her ashes which looked, in the small cream pitcher, like fragments of white shells along an Amagansett beach.

After I'd say my three lines I'd always pick a flower from somewhere else and put it on the little heap of her ashes that still remained between the marguerite (fancy word for daisy bush) and the peach colored

finally blossoming rhododendron that Mark Lindberg
had brought the night of the memorial.

Oh, I forgot to tell about the memorial.

It was a Monday night and we had it in the house.
I'd asked some of the people I knew to come by as I
wanted to have some kind of ritual but couldn't
imagine doing it in an undertaker's parlor or regular
religious trip.

Laurie was a firm believer in God, which is more
than I can say for myself. It is the unquestioning acceptance of His ways that I can't seem to get behind.
If you look at the world and even such small matters
as the genetic inheritance that was handed out to
Laurie by her actual birth parents, you have to admit
that at the very least, God is not well organized.

At any rate, Mark Lindberg, who had stayed in our
garage for a year before being called to San Diego to
drill for the Gulf War, came, bringing first a rhododendron that had not yet flowered, and then a teeny pine
seedling in a pot. Laurie's boyfriend of six years, who
she hadn't seen since the year before, didn't come, and
her friend who was in a different room at the motel
the night she overdosed, didn't come because he was
in John Muir Hospital with a bleeding ulcer.

Except for Mark Lindberg, nobody who knew her
showed up. However, as her address book and note-
book and diary were missing when we were given her
possessions, I hadn't known who to call.

When Grandpa died all the friends and neighbors
who had known him showed up. Everybody brought

flowers and the boys from Allen's band sent a huge platter of roast beef and corned beef and turkey and pastrami, with platters of potato salad and coleslaw and so many pickles that they lasted for months.

Anyhow this time at least our friends came. Jennifer came, though she hadn't known Laurie, with these wonderful little candles wrapped in tissue, and on each of them she had written words like For Healing or For Passion or For Inspiration and Mental Clarity. B.N. Duncan and Ace Backwards came with Blue, and lots of cut roses, and later on the porch I asked Blue to sing the gospel song he'd sung at Yume's memorial. Everybody had laughed when he'd sung it then, except me. I'd thought it was one of the most beautiful songs I had ever heard.

Rago came also, though it was hard to get his wheelchair up the stairs, which reminded me we should at least have a portable wooden ramp.

His attendant Mike came also, and this was a little hard for me because Mike had given Laurie grief though he certainly hadn't intended to, he'd just been doing what he thought he should and hadn't reckoned on that some people are stronger than others and some vessels are so weak that they break in the same wind a stronger vessel could withstand.

Carol came and I was so glad to see her. Six months before, after her chemotherapy, we had been terrified. But she was looking good now, and her hair was growing back. Erika came, supportive as always, uncritical and accepting.

Her parents, who had been the only friends of my husband's to have continued to care about and help us after he had died in '67, sent waves of understanding across three thousand miles and a pink azalea, frothing with bloom.

Ann came and planted two pretty plants for me and for Laurie with whom she'd had a fistfight in the years Laurie was still drinking, but who understood that had all changed, as being hooked on opiates in recent years instead of booze had quieted Laurie down totally.

Michael brought a pizza and wine and nobody quite knew what to do including me, so everyone drank wine or beer or diet Pepsi for a while and nibbled on the cheese and crackers that my other daughter Emily and her husband Joe had brought.

My third daughter was in Michigan and I hadn't wanted her to come because I thought her visit should be saved for a happier time as my other children still had a lot of anger at Laurie for ruining their childhoods. We had always been told Laurie had schizophrenia and shouldn't be raised with the girls that had been born to me. But we had adopted her before the others had been born and hadn't known what to do.

More people came including my niece Crissy and her husband John and their bright-eyed little boy, Ross. Somebody started a fire in the oven, toasting bagels, but John put it out before it got out of control. Then it started to be a bit of a blur. There wasn't much of a ceremony. I read a page or so from a book by Thomas Szasz and Milton Friedman about how the state shouldn't have the right to tell people what drugs to use, and I'd asked Mark to read the Kaddish which he did. His accent sounded different from the sounds I'd heard in my childhood but that was OK. It was comforting. Not many were Jewish and the ones who were didn't know Hebrew anyhow, so they didn't notice his mistakes.

One of my friends suddenly let out with "Amazing Grace" and Jennifer read a poem by Christina Rossetti which was so sweet and simple that it started the tears I was trying to keep down because I knew there would be no end to them. It was weird to feel like crying all the time when I knew I was supposed to *not* feel that way since everybody had solemnly assured me that Laurie was "certainly better off...and out of pain finally..." as though she had cancer or something, instead of overdosing on the cheap new heroin that had been flooding San Francisco and hooking so many people they even had an hour special on 20/20 about it, with Barbara Walters being sympathetic to a formerly straight construction worker and an intelligent loving mother who had turned into a junkie and was trying to stop.

Anyhow back to ashes, the subject that had started this whole gush of remembering which I'm trying to stop actually as it's important to get back on track and not turn morbid about this since nothing can be done about it.

So everyday I'd do a bit more in the little garden and every day I noticed that the cup of ashes I'd sprinkled above the ground had begun to disappear. It seemed strange that in less than two weeks they couldn't be seen at all.

I took this as a sign that I was supposed to focus on something else so I only stayed a minute or so where they had been sprinkled, saying my three lines of Kaddish and putting a new flower there every day.

Although I only managed to learn one line more of Kaddish I knew that wouldn't matter to Laurie, so I spent time on something I thought would have mattered to her. I put together all the home movies I'd ever taken of her and tried to arrange them in a way that would let people who saw it know that she had been in a predicament that needed the kind of help from our society that she just didn't get, and that there were lots of people like her still in the same trap who also needed help.

I figured I would finish it and it would be so strong that it would get some laws changed. I was going to send it to California State Mental Health and Hillary Clinton and my local congressman, and Senator Daniel Patrick Moynihan, who I had dated twice in high school where we had been on inter high school debating team together; and Deep Dish Cable. It was good that the ashes had worked their way into the ground and couldn't be seen anymore because I'd intended to put a teaspoon or so into the packages when I sent them but that would have been close to going off the deep end of course.

I wondered if this country was aware it was practicing a kind of genocide in regard to people who had dual diagnoses, much the same as Hitler had decided to off not only Jews but especially ones who were weak. That included the mentally ill of any racial heritage, and all who couldn't pull their weight in terms of work, like really old people and children.

Here the genocide is more subtle but you know it's still happening, since we haven't come that far since the Civil Rights movement, and people on the fringe get edged out more and more.

Every family has a bad boy. Laurie was the "bad boy." When you take such a child to a psychiatrist, you are likely to come out with a dumb label that has the word schizophrenia in it. Simple, or chronic undifferentiated, or schizoaffective, or childhood schizophrenia. In the 50s it was thought to be caused by unconscious rejection. In the 80s, after all these twin studies, they decided it was caused by some inherited genetic blip. Others thought it wasn't caused by anything, and, in fact, didn't exist.

Regarding the successive theories, I remembered that Gilda Radner used to say "If it's not one thing it's another." And I'd think of the tune—

"Hail, hail, the gang's all here
what the hell do they know *now*?"

The rest of the family had already been traumatized two decades before by a murder committed by this relative by marriage. My mom's little nephew and his father had died, so the family was terrified of any label suggesting mental illness.

This family closed itself in, for safety, in a silent tribal way, and, except for seeing Aunt Emily three thousand miles away, every few years, Laurie became a virtual outsider, carefully excluded from any thought of family function or family events for most of her life.

In terms of the ashes, at the memorial I copied the ritual that Ben Felsher had begun at Yume's memorial and passed around Laurie's last pack of Winston Lights, one of four packs I'd got her for the detox the day I'd taken her from the locked unit she had signed herself into while I was away.

Everybody lit up and coughed and there were still six cigarettes left in the pack when they all left and I sat for a while eating pretzels and crying over what had been such a messed up life, remembering how sad she had been that last year.

Through the next week I smoked one of the cigarettes each day where I had sprinkled the ashes and said the three lines of Kaddish that I was firm on and tried to get used to that I was going to have much more time and not have to worry about her any more.

Then I got heavily into work again because it's what I do, and began to make this little movie about her to try to change legislation, since I'm no good at meetings or regular political action, and am a proven coward at demonstrations.

It's a wonder I didn't get hooked on the Winston

lights or the huge bottle of phenobarbital she'd left, but I didn't, which isn't to say that I never will.

I don't understand about addiction any more than anyone else, even the experts.

I don't understand about ashes either and am not optimistic about ever understanding. For example, when we burn up or bury the bodies of people we raised, where do their souls go? Although I am dubious about visions of immortality like people walking around in heaven (I don't believe in hell at all) I am a total believer in the immortality of the *human* soul. Which probably makes me seriously inconsistent because I have no such conviction about the immortality of the soul of a spider, or even that spiders *have* souls. After the rain they wander in from the yard and I swat them left and right with no feeling at all.

Anyhow it is now May and Laurie's ashes have sifted into the ground. The only ashes I have left are those of her cigarettes and I carefully saved the butts after I'd smoked them, choking all the while, wondering what Winston regulars would be like since *these* seemed to me so strong, and luckily made me nauseous.

Next Sunday my kid brother Allen and his wife Emily are going to sprinkle the rest of Laurie's ashes around her father's stone in New York. I'd asked that something be inscribed and my sister had called an engraver who said there was plenty of room to engrave her name and dates and a quotation on his stone (her father's, not the engraver's). The only hitch was that according to cemetery rules it was against Jewish law to put more than one person on the stone and we couldn't have another stone because they would know she was there and there was supposed to be only one person to a plot.

So I told my sister to find a Catholic or Protestant engraver who wouldn't worry about breaking the Jewish law since I strongly doubted such a law existed in the Bible or the Talmud and probably had been just an interpretation by some cemetery association focused on the almighty dollar.

Then, in case it wasn't going to work out back there, I went to the trophy store in Oakland and ordered a brass plaque that had her name and dates and the inscription "Angels Keep This Child Safe."

Because try as I might to remember her as grown, and especially as the ashes, which had once been her adult body, were gone, I had begun to think of her again as the five month old child I had first seen at the adoption agency, covered with diaper rash, with frightened pleading eyes and runny nose.

I don't know what makes some people able to be so happy, and life so hard, so heartbreakingly hard, for other people. I was raised to always look at the sunny side of life and I still will. Laurie's ashes have joined the others all over the world and there are some so unmarked that there is no one to even light a Yorzheit candle for them on their birthday or the day they died, so probably I'm lucky as the little plaque can be nailed to the fence or the tree we planted for the others in 1979, and she did probably go out in a burst of white light as they say the new heroin around is all too pure.

Incidentally, for those who want to have a ball-park figure for their future, it cost eight hundred and seventy eight dollars for the minimum, to have yourself or your relative cremated, plus about another two hundred for extras, urns and things which you actually only use once. I'm not sure what my brother will do with Laurie's when it's empty, it wasn't exactly a beautiful urn though made of respectably sturdy brass or copper, I'm uncertain which.

Today I remembered reading about the Neptune Society in the *Guardian*. We had phoned another by mistake thinking it was that one, either because the name was close or the cops recommended it, I'm not sure which.

What the article had been about was that when poor people were buried by the county, it cost three hundred and forty nine dollars for relatives to redeem their ashes. The county used someone called the Neptune Society, so in the next issue someone from the Neptune Society wrote back saying they were troubled because they were supplying cremations for poor people to the city for one hundred dollars (which was barely cost) as a public service, and the County was making a hearty profit from each of these transactions.

So of course someone from the county wrote back citing assorted expenses such as salaries of those assigned to execute the enormous amount of red tape the county had allowed to accumulate and

cited figures, as every County office has been trained
to cite figures, showing how they are running the
ashes-to-ashes dust-to-dust program at a loss.

And so, coming to the end of my thoughts about
ashes, as probably the world is getting colder or hot-
ter or whatever that Nobel Prize winner predicted, I
resolved to have a happy life in the future, for whatever time is left, and be glad that Laurie had been free
to experience all the major emotions of life and even
the events though not family ones.

Then I resolved not to sink into the kind of sad-
ness that had floated through me like miasmic L.A.
air when they'd weighed the small package I was
mailing to my brother, and it had come to exactly
what the lady at the agency had said Laurie weighed
when she was born.

Blood

GUESS WHAT? I remained haunted by the thought of ashes for a very long time and was then sent into a new kind of purgatory when my thoughts went from ashes to blood after I had spoken to Barton.

It was impossible to forget the way blood had impacted on Laurie's life. Barton hadn't known Laurie had died and when I told him he said wearily—though with an almost childlike wonder—that people had not taken his art seriously until, suffering from AIDS, he had begun to work with blood (his own) using it, as well as the ashes of his friends as art supplies.

Maybe because it was a time when I couldn't express the way I felt directly since everyone around was still saying things like "she's better off now, out of her suffering," it seemed at that moment that a huge bloodstain, a bloodstain the size of a house, seemed to have run down over her whole existence, almost obliterating it.

I remembered—and these memories appeared as out-of-focus images, the tiny cuts and scrapes she'd received as a child—that every child receives. How she'd cry as I'd come running with the mercurochrome and bandaids, hug her and wipe away the blood. Blood always scared her. The smallest trickle suggested imminent death. When she was thirteen and began to menstruate, despite the thousand times I explained that periods are normal, she would shriek in terror at the beginning of her periods. "I'm bleeding," she would say helplessly, never remembering the reassurance that it was ok, there was nothing wrong.

The single thing that most differentiated her from her peers as she got older was that through her entire life she never was able to do what most people do. Until I would literally hand her the sanitary napkin or tampon, it would never occur to her that there was a way to prevent the blood from streaming down her leg, and that most females past the age of fourteen were accustomed to using this way. Laurie's uncontained menses poured out regularly on mattresses wherever she slept.

After many years she'd finally learned to use sanitary napkins, but it was always only after being frightened by first seeing a bloodstained sheet or blood on her clothes.

Her horror about blood became mine one day as I

stared at her face, arms and shirt totally drenched with blood. She'd come in after having been beaten up by a boyfriend, her face a white mask of panic. She'd spoken in a fast pressured voice I'd never heard. Her always present need to be with someone, anyone, to replace the loneliness, led her sometimes to encounters with truly dangerous people.

Anyhow after so many doctors had labeled her mentally ill, the family became frightened thinking she might turn "violent." Indeed she had been a violent child—up to the very last time they saw her, her sisters had remained afraid of her. Yet in those last years her violence had ebbed, I have no idea why.

No one would give her another chance, they had all been too hurt by the past. Her grandmother, unable to ever forget the sight of blood-spattered walls the night her small nephew had been murdered by a stepmother who was later diagnosed as paranoid schizophrenic, tried to help. Unfortunately the last time she saw Laurie was still at a time she was drinking heavily and was therefore totally unreachable. Later, twelve step programs helped her with her drinking problem though not with the equally problematic need for so many pills that she remained non functioning. In her whole life she had held a job at a pizza place for two weeks, one minding retarded children in a playground for a week, and telemarketing (asking questions over the phone) for almost three weeks. That was her vocational history. They all ended specifically when she got her period and the old terror at seeing blood returned.

So when Barton said he was making his new art pieces from his own blood and called the exhibit "Lethal Weapons," my mind leaped, as it does sometimes when we're caught in a cross current of free flying associations. And the next word that came after blood in Winston Churchill's unforgettable speech during World War II (not long before her then soldier father had watched the severed leg of his best friend spurt bright arterial blood in the Black Forest in the Ardennes) was sweat. Blood, sweat and tears, he had said. So of course the next word that had come into sharp focus when I thought "blood" was "sweat."

Sweat

Laurie had always interpreted sweat as another sign of impending destruction of body. Again, however often I explained that sweat was a natural body function under certain conditions, she would whisper, in a state of total desperation "Ma, I'm starting to dissolve. Look how the juice is running out of me."

Except when drinking or when having a period, she was fastidious, obsessive in fact, about wanting her body to be clean. A few moments of sweating would cause her to run and shower. She regarded sweat as scary, first step in the process of dissolution during which the liquid would pour down, she would be a kind of wrung out plastic wrapping for a bit, and then life would be over. It was this process she was afraid of always, and that's why I'm grateful that the white light in which she must have died suddenly, had spared her waiting for the kind of event she feared.

It was odd how my other children usually treated sweat with the measure of respect it probably deserves. In their eyes, and the rest of the family including me, sweating was something you did when you had made an effort you could be proud of, or it was just a process that simply happened when it was hot or you had done a bunch of healthy exercise, or you'd "accomplished something." Laurie never knew the positive connotation of Churchill's famous speech. To the end of her life, sweat for her remained a kind of little death, the beginning of the end,where whatever was inside would begin to ooze out until there would be nothing left.

And so, waking to a cold sweat a hundred nights after Laurie had died, I would tiptoe in to another room, open an album of childhood pictures, and wonder: is there anything I could have done to make it all end differently? Any magic word I could have said? This dual diagnosis stuff—was it a way to categorize a soul in torment, who inflicted her ongoing anxiety on everyone around, especially her little sisters, and who saw as through an inaccessible bakery window the realities we all take for granted, that stayed obscure and glassed off from her always?

Winston Churchill had ended his memorable sentence with the word Tears. Blood, sweat and tears. It rolls off the tongue like a prayer.

Tears

IT WAS EASY TO STOP THINKING about sweat, while sitting in a cool backyard I had begun to turn into a second garden. But to think about tears, that was another matter—to think about that would be to open the floodgates of hell again. Oddly, the harder I tried not to think about it, the more memories of tears rushed in like the little boy in Holland had taken his finger out of the hole in the dike.

Whose tears? Laurie's, mine, her sisters', the man in the street who always asks, not for a quarter but for seventeen cents? In other words, everybody.

A baby's occasional tears are as normal as a young girl's blood at menarche, or sweat after pruning an overgrown shrub. But everything is quantitative and I started to remember how right from the start Laurie's tears had come a hundred times more frequently than those of the children born to me.

I thought of the many days and nights I had held her, rocked her in my arms the year we brought her home before the final adoption papers had been signed, and how nothing I could do, extra warmth, a bottle, a change of diaper, a hug, could stop her tears.

Those tears, in my dreams, slide down her baby cheeks without stopping, forever maybe. Nothing could ease the cries of anguish that came from her then, until I felt a failure at mothering, and in regard to her, still do. Doctors said nothing was wrong physically, but something that caused her pain was there from the time I first saw her at five months, to the time she died. Tears throughout her whole life? Yes, that was the most obvious part of the mysterious illness they called childhood schizophrenia. That and the utter inability to be happy for long.

In the last year she frequently lost control of her bladder even when she was totally sober. I didn't know if this was because of nervousness or a kidney problem—she'd been checked in hospital so it was likely the first. I can still hear her say, "Ma, my bladder is crying again."

Water is water wherever it flows from, but sometimes she would both cry and leak urine at the same time and I didn't know how to comfort her.

So I remembered (probably getting the facts wrong—facts don't seem as important to me lately as they used to) the Hans Christian Anderson fairy story in which the tears of somebody—I can't recall who—melted the sliver of ice in Gerda the Ice Maiden's heart. In that story tears were good. So, shivering at five AM I tried to catch them with a piece of toilet tissue before they faded into my pajama top. Of course it didn't work—tears are as hard to hold onto as laughter. So I closed my eyes but no more tears would come and the sliver of ice that felt lodged in my heart is still there.

What is Dual Diagnosis

THE TERM DUAL DIAGNOSIS is frequently used by doctors and insurance companies to describe people who have both a chemical dependency problem and also a mental disorder .

The diagnosis suggests problems that are both psychological and biological, implying that there is a long-standing difficulty that exists in the relationship between the sufferer and his environment. It involves a severe inability to function, suggesting that the disturbance is not only in the relationship between the person and society, and that the difficulties are not temporary or passing. The DSM-III-R, a diagnostic text for psychiatrists and insurance companies that can perpetuate as many problems as it describes, defines substance abuse (one part of the diagnosis) as a maladaptive pattern of use that has persisted for at least one month or has occurred repeatedly over a longer time period.

In retrospect it is clear to me, and also everyone who knew her, that Laurie suffered through all her adult life from this progression into an even graver disability than that occasioned only by her "mental illness" which was really an identifiable distortion of perception causing her to feel almost constant anxiety.

When continuing behavior causes heavy physical, psychological, social or occupational problems or when there is repeated use in situations that may be dangerous, we are told that functioning is maladaptive. The Diagnostic Manual, often inaccurate, is used mostly as a quick easy way for doctors to submit bills or reach a quick understanding with other doctors, plus insurance billing. We find the abuse diagnosis is more likely to apply to those who have only recently started using addictive substances or who use substances less likely to be associated with withdrawal symptoms. Yet it was our family's unhappy experience that substance abuse became a big part of Laurie's routine, causing heavier problems in terms of functioning, than had existed before.

The main feature of what is called substance abuse is continued use despite knowing it is going to cause trouble and unhappiness rather than pleasure. The standard criteria for this diagnosis requires that symptoms occur repeatedly. It also agrees that the person given the diagnosis cannot help accelerated use for longer periods than intended, along with heavy painful withdrawal symptoms that make it impossible to fulfill obligations or carry out plans. People with this problem need to continue the addiction even when confronting danger. Someone suffering in this way shows an inability to function in a way he or she wants to. A troubled addict is not able to cut down or do anything much beyond hunting for the substance needed to score. The diagnosis usually involves blackouts and frequent binges, along with heavy withdrawal symptoms showing at least three of the following: use of greater amounts for longer periods than intended; persistent desire or unsuccessful attempts to cut down or stop; large amount of time spent obtaining the substance or recovering from the use; painful withdrawal symptoms. Often former goals are abandoned because of continued use of whatever the person is hooked on. It causes other personal problems, such as: tolerance or the need to take increasing amounts of the substance to achieve the same effect; use despite crippling withdrawal symptoms, and continuing even in the face of danger. Those given this diagnosis often can't function in today's world in a way that could make them feel fulfilled.

Before Laurie began to drink heavily, she wrote poetry and spent much time drawing. After long-term use of assorted addictive substances, from too much alcohol to too many pills, she could barely do anything at all, managing only to fill her most basic physical needs, and that with considerable pain.

Recent years show a substance abuse epidemic so widespread that media reports are still alarming. More people are using dangerous "hard" drugs, like crack, speed, and heroin, and at a younger age.

Like thousands of others, Laurie's lifetime anxiety made her more vulnerable to chemical dependence. People with a history of major depression or anxiety disorder seem to have double the risk of the average population for chemical dependency. Chemical abuse rates causing non-functioning and trouble are more than fifty percent in young chronically ill mental patients.

People with a dual diagnosis are often in pain. The situation is one where the whole problem is greater than the sum of its parts, since each disorder makes things worse. The confused person becomes more confused, the hostile person more hostile, and suicide can happen. Those having trouble being accepted because of their head problems run into even more trouble when they get hooked on crack or too much booze and heavy painkillers. More hospitalizations are needed, emergency rooms are needed much more often. When I tried to get help for Laurie, without a huge amount of money it was impossible to get the kind of decent living situation along with treatment that could have made a difference.

The questions facing those who try to help are these: Are the person's difficulties in dealing with reality caused more by the addiction, the head trouble, or both? Will the person be helped more in a mental health or straight chemical dependency program? Does he or she need a dual diagnosis program and if so, how can one be found and how can friend, doctor, or family member tell which ones are good? And finally, how can the addict himself or herself know where to go to get real help?

So many times we faced this dilemma, getting a

thousand referrals to places that sounded okay in description, but really weren't. For many years, when I tried to get help for Laurie I was faced with shrinking resources that had everything to do with budget cuts in health care. When all referrals were used up (lots of the resources had closed) there was still no real help in sight.

Possibilities of help center around rules of insurance coverage. In twentieth century America, when it comes to help for people on the fringe of society, society itself is often the nut case.

Chemical dependency has been described as a disease. This view has been accepted lately since it relates to a genetic problem in that people who have it find that the body doesn't get rid of the substance anywhere as quickly as people who don't and can thereby be "social drinkers" with the ability to stop short of damage. The disease unfortunately is chronic—it does not go away, it is progressive—it worsens with time—and it often leads to death.

In spite of more than thirty years of this concept, many professionals and certainly the general public, don't believe it or understand how chemical dependency can be a disease. The behavior of an alcoholic or addict can be so upsetting to those around that the end result is often rage along with despair.

It breaks my heart to remember those moments when I shouted at Laurie, blaming her constant difficulties on "selfishness." I think now that the cards were stacked against her. During World War Two a soldier would say "that bullet had his number." I think it was like that with her.

During most of Laurie's life, people tended to see her as "bad" instead of "sick." An approach that treats chemically dependent, anxious people like "sick people trying to get better" not "bad people trying to get good" would have helped.

The "disease process" recovery model provides support for people with Laurie's problem without so much blame.

This view perceives the addict or alcoholic as never "recovered," but always "recovering." The disease is lifelong. For this reason it is really important for those with this double problem to know about cross tolerance and addiction. One of the terrifying features of true alcoholism is a metabolic tolerance. This refers to the body's adaptation response to the presence of alcohol. Those who have the genetic factor known as the "disease" find their bodies tolerate large doses of the substance without experiencing the effects associated with increased use. The symptom of tolerance is one way to distinguish a social drinker from an alcoholic.

We often hear "recovering" alcoholics discuss how they were prescribed a minor tranquilizer for a panic disorder or used other chemicals when not drinking, only to find they had now become addicted to this new drug. This situation is known as cross addiction. Addicts and alcoholics, particularly those with dual diagnoses, often switch their "drug of choice" to other classes of chemicals outside the nervous system depressant category in an attempt to self medicate their long standing emotional pain.

They soon see that their body processes all chemicals differently from the non-addicted person. The liver holds alcohol and opiates longer. We have to understand and accept that a need for certain substances, in people with the genetic predisposition, is a overwhelming urge, more significant to the addict than relationships, money, food and shelter.

When the emotional roller coasters of head problems such as major depression, bipolar illness, and schizophrenia is added, those agonies of withdrawal even beyond the physical suffering, need to be recognized.

It's impossible to forget a fragment of home movies I ran a month after my daughter's death. In it I heard her say, "Do you see these scars? (Referring to injuries received when an alcoholic boyfriend had beat up on her.) My psychic pain is worse." As I watched her eyes fill and heard her voice quaver, I knew that to be true.

No Help in Sight

THE MEMORY OF THE "BAD" OLD DAYS—of huge, pitifully understaffed state asylums packed with terrified patients—still influences our thinking today. Some authorities insist there is no alternative for the most severely ill.

Everyone agrees that the quality of community-based care must be improved. Only taxpayers aren't ready to foot the bill. The last few decades of experience has taught us that deinstitutionalization, if it is ever to succeed, will require at least as much staff and at least as much spending as long-term institutional care.

An 'aggressive case-management' approach used by a few progressive programs, for example, relies on especially hard working counselors and low case-loads if possible. If we were to say what the biggest problem still is regarding these dual diagnoses that make society show thumbs down, it's that the American public just doesn't care.

What can solve this? What can help? When we see a sick homeless person freaking out or simply suffering on the street, we look away. To this day

STRANGER ON THE PLANET: *The Small Book of Laurie*

nobody knows what schizophrenia really is, indeed if it exists, since all ways of talking about it are impressions drawn from the disciplines of medicine, art, psychology, religion, or what have you.

"We begin by saying that schizophrenia is constitutional, something between a talent and a handicap. It is a talent in the sense that people who have it are able to notice things that other people can't, but a handicap in that they notice too much and overreact and fret about all of it." In some cases mental illness is clearly not a myth—yes, Thomas Szasz, it certainly does exist—(though the injustices and conflicts of our society play a strong fierce role in increasing negative symptoms). Still controversial are its physical and biological aspects, though most people today acknowledge a genetic component. "To the extent that it is a disease, schizophrenia is like epilepsy, in that it is mainly manifested in alterations of behavior and consciousness."

It requires warm hearted planning with family, friends, and others. It needs a network of supporters, the more the better, for the person being bombarded with symptoms is in an Intensive Care Unit of the heart.

We want a society that encourages compassion and provides ways to help avoid reality situations like having no decent place to live, that lead to "hot spots" and symptom recurrence.

What we want to avoid is the social stigma and lack of real help that taints all efforts to make life more bearable for those already dealt a losing hand by nature.

All I can do for my daughter now is try to make this clear. If I do, maybe some of the others still trapped by the hurricane in their head, might have more of a fighting chance.

If I Married a Cowboy

poetry by Laurie Burch

If I married a cowboy
would the whale shoot forth in the
sea of glowing amber?
Would the green-eyed Lion still
smile gently at me as his tail flowed
to the breeze of the palm trees?

Uncarved legends to be left on the beach.
Wandering in ancient eyes, weary-dust covered
    fact
In my solitary confusion I felt
your hand and where it comes
to rest, you take my head in
both of your hands and into my
soul you breathe love and comfort.
And then, the lion
and seagull, the baby deer
and even the teeny weeny
wooden toy houseboat go forth in
the meadow
and rejoice
in a secret clearing

When I was as young as you
I lived in the cereal boxes
and communed with all the multi-colored
corn and wheat.
I kicked
the corn balls and bounced around
the checks of wheat
My curiosity found me inside
the toys marveling at the
glittering glistening objects
of splendor How they worked
what made them work
collecting them too at times
But now I only dream of
their remoteness.
Their distance is now meaningless
the magic is buried
that era is past
and sifted through time
into complex womanhood

A young bull in spring
nothing seems to faze
him not anything
the meadows daisies remain
undisturbed
in his presence
His mind is far away
His dream-like fantasy state
appears him to be idle
He is really aware of the
grass under him on which he
rests.
He is at odds with others
and his mate
occasionally he'll give a snort
and thicken his head
He bats his tail lazily in
the sun
Even the smallest of
creatures know him
For his public relations
are good
He is content

Jackrabbit bounds thru
the branches. His huge
hind legs enable him to
powerfully leap
when he takes off
from the refuge of
a cluster of tumble weed
the landscape
seems a good camouflage
with the exception of
only a few flat seconds
of blurred back tipped
ears and fluffy tail.
High thru the air
He is constantly on the run.

He runs and runs
not knowing where he
goes
instinct carries him
through ditches, across
fields, beneath
bridges, over aqueducts
gradually his space
becomes narrowed
and is in
perspective, his choice
is lessened
less alternative
renders his direction frantic
he is being
out in the boom
of a technological
revolution and
electronic era.

To my dear beloved deceased friend and brother Don

the snow was melting
into summer's soft misty touch
golden mountains are proud to have
had you tread upon them
At the base of the mountains
in a silent separate spot
there you were!
I seized my heart
Your broken body beneath
the great wall
You gave
me a charm bracelet with hearts on it.
Shock and horror engulfed me
I could not cry
I see your body now
absent in spirit like I had
never seen before.
I wanted to run over to you
and comfort you
But now,
you could not feel
even my kiss.

at 7 A.M. on Pier IV
you can see me sketching
the great colossal phallic
symbol
that is impregnating the
stratosphere
with its vile, toxic fumes
It's off somewhere in
the mist near New Jersey
My mind flows against
the current
to my friends held in the
bondage of Dr. Seuss'
Marble chambers.

Fort Tryon Park
once the courting grounds
of the wild beast and the elk

Circumstance travel
agent. Grandma is late
with check. Because of four
days time after the first fares
went up on the 1st.
Maybe can go there.
airlines. Maybe
should postpone trip until
after Grandpa's operation.

I. Plateau of Innocence

Oh island of childhood
that is so far away
and yet still at home
Cuddled warm and snug
still in her arms
Near a warm hearth
and warm living room
glowing luminescent
with every evening's fire

with no conception
of time
I staggered around
in a daze
a passerby would stare
at me quizzically
and a little voice would
cry out
Sir, can you spare some change?

Stairways of sorrow
rooms occupied
though empty
Figures revolving
whirling in black
they do not want to come back
Have you ever seen
the spirits Floating
around Telegraph Ave. at
night?
Children amorphous
disintegrated souls
Roar unmeasured
time void
Stairways of sorrow
rooms occupied

and if you care and
still have compassion
in you
you will never dare
to tread upon this
God forsaken turf
unless you
infallibly
(without fail) expect
to change it.

Don't worry mommy
it's only a poem
Directed at nobody
it just describes
Union Square and
the City.

Mommy is someone who talks
about the flowers
and the little girl sitting beside her
wants to pick them
She talks about the little mousey
that just ran in the hole in the fence
She takes me for walks
to the zoo
and buys me ice cream
and helium balloons
she takes me home about 5
and feeds me all sorts of delicacies
from Bohack and A & P
that she herself can hardly afford
for I know she loves me dearly
She reads me stories
about the little red choo-choo and
Grimms fairy tales
time has past
but Mommy is the same
She is always young her beauty
and kindness will never fade
for it lasts forever as her love.
I'll never forget
the Brooklyn eagle, Saturday morning oatmeal
chocolate cookies,
the cement sandbox, with the little
blue pails, thirteen white kitty-cat tails
now—everyday—in the sunshine
you can see me lying down with my eyes closed
waiting for Mommy

We went thru a
reality in a modern
Hi-rise, we found
a little broken down
Mexican shanty
dark green splintery
and on the outside wood
and oh so very old
inside bedroom had no
door the last thing
way one room the
Mexicans were the only
ones with a dim past
share house share shower
right by front door 1 bath
3 single beds in living room area

there was a G.I. honky
in the woodstock pile
the young men, spoke
enthusiastically about their
superiors.
At that time I anxiously
awaited my entrance into
the outside world. I would
emerge an adult. Peer
acquaintances had left
prematurely, escaping into the
night. They were last seen
crossing the railroad
tracks on the far corner of the school.
A new
dimension was revealed
broken in the
kind of reform school
I was glad
for them.

about nine years later
the boy appeared
again. This time
he was grown-up,
penniless, ragged,
and alone. We recognized
each other instantly, but
I knew in only a short
time I would have to leave
and abandon the memory forever.

In dream state I try
to touch the highest
plane of human existence
but sometimes I
just have to work on
everyday reality problems.

So sock out
creature of
romantic legend,
and majestic
historical lore.
I wanted to follow
the pied piper
maybe he would send
me straight
to Robin Hood.
But was it true?
The coming
brought deeper
disillusion
accumulated through years.
October looked like
bran flakes and I
missed the spring.
Getting back to summer.

and glimmering
like a long gimlet
a partially darkened
martini glass
with the subtle
suggestion of
green flakes of fleeting

colored lights
disappearing,
vanishing in squiggles
my coffee was a warm toffee
colored
Hi there, toffee-colored coffee.
Then a lady
curls in a funny way.
She radiated goodness
and her life was a
warm family life in
brown gold and topaz.
She always left you with
the feeling of being peaceful.
Dream of my mother.

there were periods when I did nothing.
a vacuum consumed me
stare into space
occasionally a thought would
enter my mind
and then leave.
smoke rings formed
then vanished
into previous philosophies
taken for granted
distractions are none
in this realm
and the dragon knows
he must stay

return to the world
the journey of satisfaction
fulfillment a must
cry out in ghetto pain
sailor's trouble seeking their best
foreign town of heartbreak
heartbreaks
but always blown in direction
of the same
the people flow cattle-like
no one knows my name
Easter blows the Waikiki surf
and rises to meet the sun head-on
solar collision
spiritual engulfing
danger, love, pain, and hunger
is the feeling of ice
that just can't thaw

diamond head to kona
the palm tree
traveling down diamond highway
with a backpack, and
bloody lip
crying out for something
that I never really wanted.

up in the hills
overlooking the Bay, I saw
an aircraft carrier
slightly glide along the
placid waters far below
the steep
terraced landscape.
It shone from the
gentle illumination of
the morning sun.
I could see
down the slope from
house to house and
highest my strategic
point, far from the sea
below.
I woke beside my brand
new husband.
He was still asleep.
I touched the front curl
on the middle of his forehead.
He began to stir sleepily and
slowly opened one eye.
I smiled at him and felt calm.

I found out
he was a
December
and while
Charley was looking
over the
checks I told him
to wash-up

He started getting
playful and
squirted sprayed me
with some of his
cologne
I coughed and
choked.

"How can you talk
to a falcon that
doesn't fly."
I have more
hang-ups then the
taxi driver with
a wife and 10 mouths to
feed. Some dried
out, flaky, old
soap opera."
yeack!
Who needs it?

143

I only said that
I wanted out. He choked me.
I tried
to work and find job
I can't cope
with Silicon Valley
worst part of California
for my particular
make-up
not feasible

give up if under
pressure or fury
competing with a group of people. Head still
    hurts.
turn into a hooker

We are still inside our house
that lies one side up
covered by brush
the other side juts out over the landscape
we speak in platitudes
until that to is shattered
by a noise outside
outside there in the unknown
we can hardly see it
it is too dark, perhaps the darkest
night of the year
the whiteness of our house
with trimmings of
crystal and jewel are our
only hope and our only refuge
from the darkness
for we are afraid of the darkness
those two out there whoever they are
cannot come inside for they are two
evil musicians two raving minstrels
that terrorize lives like ours.

7 openings I'm calling on
Hello, I'm representing
Charlie
I'm Mr. G's personal
secretary.
Mr. G in seeking
employment as a software
systems programmer.
Mr. G is seeking a programming
position, in a state of the
art, innovative
company, which would
recognize and reward
work in the areas of
real-time multi-tasking
systems.

User friendly

operator interface
software procurement
and artificial
Mr. G is presently
working for Dysan Corporation
writing systems and applications
software, for
diskettes developed at Dysan.

This involved
both in house real-time
operating systems
developed in house in
assembly language
and it involves a
real-line multi-tasking
executive developed by etc.
there's a tag
on this bull's ear

"Dear Tony," Dear Tony,"
there's a tag on this bull's ear.
like his brother Tony,
Charley doesn't really like women either.

passion of black
you pseudo bleak blonde
brown you twinkle
I'll trick you too
but first call
the exterminator
blonde you're obscure and
you want something I am not
equipped to give at present
children, children come forth
go away pain I love you!
acrylics,
holders—I'll take them from
you and your license to practice
aggression, stained, washed, faded
memories, tears,
fusion + fusion is
confusion, 10:15

There are 1,000
girls, hungry for you.
Many that deeply
and desperately desire ;you.
But they are neither right
for you nor are you right
for them.
I may have to
stand in line for you again
waiting till you go through
all of them.

Alienated identity
Doena Worthieimer
Rusty Louvenstcin
Robin Gadden
Khutsen Sorenson
Laurie Helmhaltz
Ezra Schmulawitz
Micheala Kearney

Yellow-orange turtle neck
cyclone
Swirl-Swirl pull
sharp-rap-bite spite
I, like you
can slight, without fight.
nights have no division
Days have no flight
promises are never
overlooked.
Days monoxide microcomputer
Night—not flight
day—not suspension of
delay
I went through the windshield.
Go away headache.

I stood on a stone
scared with back feet tightly
together. The stone was surrounded
by dry patches of golden bleached out
stained-glass-tumble weed in every
point of view.
And direction around me the
strange horizon ahead.
Immediately following the car
accident to the sunny mesa
plateau sunny warmth almost
live desolation feet like
nowhere this consciousness would
find myself forced to walk
a pass through a long pitch black tunnel
I might find myself
abruptly in an inner city walk
beautiful, surrealistic
mural of the crucifiction.

motions through which I go are mechanic
moving machinery lost of soul
void of feeling unable to panic
death has no dominion and life has no role.

not to want not to need only to exist
impaled in the bands of apathy
stacked not high or low
with nothing left
mask of a clown warm sad or happy

remembrance in wonder to wake or relive
anyheart kind or sincere face
can behold that loss, not ready to live longer.
(unfinished)

My early journals
I found a space of
rambling and scattered
incoherence. Too many
days were held
unaccountable.
He didn't mean to throw me out the window.
The car turned over twice.

1741 San Lorenzo Avenue
I saw a movie
Home Box Office
back roads
same main character
as Coal Miner's Daughter
I so much identified
with it (my past life or one of them)
I opted for it again
I am bitter very
stuck in the mud
cranky Charley. I view
Charley as a husband still
but I need
excitement, fun, adventure.

Fierce competition
illegal aliens
get the jobs before me.
I feel bitter because they
were stolen out from me
If I didn't marry
I would join the Armed Forces
Following recovery of course.
When I went through the windshield
My forehead hit the highway.
He says it will go away
if I drink herb tea.
My mother said sue
(he was fixing his plants in the back of the car)
The car turned over twice.
He laughed at her.

The Chatanooga
Choo Choo whipped past green
countryside (I ride Bart
practically everyday). When my
subconscious is active it
absorbs daytime-life processes.
a river runs slowly thru the
lush Tennessee greenery, but the
trains view the river
like a great mass of pubic hair.
the water itself is hidden
concealed by
a lighter green
thin line twists it's way thru
the landscape. I am moving past.
my thoughts cannot stop.
Head pounds
when the train finally stops
my thoughts are amorphous
They have no borders or boundaries
through the eye of a hawk
a cruel reflection of
death descending
on my desert shadow
at dawn
tiny roads diminishing
to private lines
that disappearing
and reappearing
to fuse centrifugally

a second to be alone
a minute to be alone
an hour to be alone
sometimes cherished
sometimes sad
glassy streets
caught up in a mirror
that reflects my fear
of the street life
from that corner to this
corner
What does it all mean?
a wave or a vibe that
radiates another world
when I came here I was
young, tender and
unassuming but you
taught me the jargon of
the streets
and dropped bread
crumbs at my feet

Something taught me to be
gregarious, although
I'm naturally not.
My private world
holds an abundance
of fascination most
people don't want to
share my world.
When I meet someone
I'm usually too
inhibited to share the
realm of my subconscious.
When I'm sure of
love for me,
I open up but it's
taken awhile. I've
always been like that.
Isn't everyone?

We both burn to share
Like the bursting tide
of our soul in mourning
we extend reach
but don't always touch.
Secrets you harbor
I may exhibit
you aren't sure of your
feelings
you try
resting your head on
my lap.

Over abundance
surplus population
of Valley teenyboppers
jealous, bitter
homicidal torture
fantasies-steal jobs
pretty
Inferiority complex
1. Weary girl
2. Young man
3. (22-24 approx.)

Set back in the north wood
I stand at the site of a great ancient fortress
It is nearing morning
the ruins behind reflect the Alamo
crumbling and standing
covered by a great army
once lead by a concentration
strength, valor, fierce involuntary battle
then the trail of a high concentration of spirits
in a small space.
The marine pushed the flag forward.

My dog a timberwolf
german shepherd cross bred
set off one day
for a hard unknown.

courage bravery guts plus no man
once in the high country
I would see the mountains
looking in the misty horizon
smell the air cold and Alpine
hint of winter green fragrance
subtly permeated consciousness.

with all its
flashing lights
and razzle-dazzle
along the commercial
strip could
be found mostly
big-time hustle
now and then in other
paths of the city
the Disco Inferno
A famous gay district
hand -out browed
with business
Beyond the boundaries
of the lake emanated
an invisible radiation
forces
So powerful and yet
invisible.
The city smoldered
with immeasurable heat
and sizzled out each rampart.

It was a smoldering
old, old consciousness
which generated fright.

Being in a bomb
at high noon
waiting for a
sound to start
illusionary shells
bursting in mid-area
somewhere off on
an alien horizon
all's quiet
all's still. The accident is over.
They take me to the hospital.
I remember 1979 but everything seems
        different.
seven lay dead.
the seventh one
I tried to nurse back
to life.
after the war my
buddy tried
to see me
safely back
to headquarters
but the train stopped
in Saint Louis
and I got off

After 1979
The headache hardly ever went away.
a feeling
how to go inside-out
strong involuntary urge
to suck tongue
Scare episodes
Severe anxiety
tension, agitation
short attention
mind flooded with
thoug ts rising through so
quickly that it is impossible
to capture one
disruptive sleeping
patterns, tendencies
to not sleep properly
trouble falling asleep
since out of hospital
sleeping patterns altered

my "sour grapes" attitude I
acquired through the pain.
I am in reality, a true loser.
Going back to a seemingly
not so distant past, I remember
and see quite clearly the
high hill plateau I will
transcend to upon my death.
I was there only (like in a
dream) for a short time
In the same way I
was in the ground so quickly this
was all fragmented and
hard to piece together. I too
became channeled into this
realm not of sleepy time
beyond life. I saw a desert city
I saw a city distorted by
distance and by heat

Lines of the hopeful end
amorphous forms
having bland lines
float through liquid brain
cool not cold
warm not hot
peace
above the skirmishes on the ground
four black rubber walls
eye in the middle
solitary
don't want to leave the thick sweet fluid
no need to breathe
brain wants—body has—
automatic
all enclosing
end of thought.

Up the down staircase
down the up staircase
there is no up and there is no down
"the hawk" he has his
and thinks he is
sharp and quick as a whip
His delusions are destructive toward
others and negatively charged

or bring forth total destruction
not alienation
only unity
Lex - Park = mom side H+S+
Ft. Hamilton Parkway, NY.
Donald Duck as opposed to regression

Pleasures of the triangle
Lemon pastry melts
into wax umbrella vendors
and the heart of
the deep purple
can't be found

a powerful fleet
drive and steer it to highest
potential, "all these
dopey secretions
to face each new morning."
I give up! But not really.
Everything is either
automatic or instant.
How can one enjoy?
Here we go round the
mulberry bush

right now, I feel indifferent, pacified, unusually
    calm,
down (even) but with 100% of all my senses, and
    a
little bit confused (as always), secure, insecure
sure, and very doubtful, calm, strong and
    helpless,
calm, cold and I don't like it and can't do
    anything
about it, sick, calm, something is coming up hot
    and
turbulent, explosive, I'm feeling the calm before
    the storm.

in extreme pain
felt like I was
jumping out
state of panic
facial muscular
twitches
so anxiety riddled my
mind would turn off
(revert back to a previous
paragraph)
4 or 5 hours
to achieve a minimal
but light sleep
wide awake no
hang-over or feelings of
drunkenness
moderate dizziness
I feel like a fish out
of water
our marriage has
taken a turn for the
worse
I want to live where
I can be happy
My husband is denying
me my constitutional
rights

passion of black
you pseudo bleak blonde
brown you twinkle
I'll trick you too
gray stay but first call
the exterminator
Blonde you're obscure and
you want something I can not give.
Not equipped to grieve at present
children, children come forth
go away pain I love you!
The car turned over just out of Texas.
acrylics, ponytail holders.
I'll take them from
you and your license to practice
aggression, stained, washed, faded
memories, tears, fusion + fusion is
confusion 10:15

Experiment

Pregnant female cockroach
about to give birth
moves tweezers
trying to get out escape
from jar but unable
incapacitated due to very
heavy with egg larvae
Blow on mother at bottom
of jar see flattened herself
against the bottom
Egg sac is protruding
9/10 of the way out
of cockroach will leave
it soon
2:30 A.M.
Myrtle is giving birth

Experiment II

I. Egg case
I. Egg case was laid by
unidentified mother
who abandoned after discharge

II. Dead mother necro-nancy
necromancy nacto force
egg case out by means of
foreign substance. (Fork)
squeezed egg case out of
cockroach abdomen.

1. goes in back of statue-
egg case from unidentified mother

2. is going in front of statue to
get some visual impression of
mother's breast

Friday before the Vietnam War
started, I was listening
to the radio. My world was
still not quite innocent and I hadn't
formed any presumptions or
type-images through mental
embittered experiences.
Identify Alice in Wonderland
falling through the rabbit hole
before in essence it is the
symbolic journey of my long
fall from innocence.
The times here and
now are much different.
Vietnam is long over,
new sense of self awareness,
feeling of being gypped or
cheated by my present husband
the fork I chose at
19, a turning point
in my life.

When the war was going
on I was still too young to
understand things.
Concepts were still obscured
and my whole identity still
seemed quite
after I started to
know more I felt cheated
I don't know why.

In the courtyard the
morning was quietly
illuminated by the
sunny warmth of summer
there was a spiritual stillness
new outside my
window and
by the door of the chapel.
Someone greater than any human was watching,
    healing,
comforting

Very depressing
shack surrounded by muck.
a large moat of
mud or few
yards of road
possibly in San Jose
Texas
next door
light and the long
low low alley to bars
the kind they have in
this shabby shanty
an old truck pulled up.
A man with brilliant red
hair and freckles got out I
was for coming on strong but
I didn't care
I didn't seem to notice
too much in pain from the headache
distinguish the two.
I asked—invited
him to join me for a
drink at Manny's
at the local bar a block
away.
he seemed to comply
I woke up.

I could readily
identify the accident,
pain, embittered by my
previous experiences.
I was in a sense,
falling through the
rabbit hole. In
essence, it was the
start
of my long fall
from innocence.

that 19 or 20 year
old boy bumped
into me in the elevator
and called me retard
and obscene names
and threatened
to beat me up.
I moved here
because I wanted
peace but
most of the valley
is filled literally
riddled with folks
ready to
rip you off or
beat you up

by the way where was I?

and yet slightly
up center and
partially beneath
my anonymous eye.
I can't even remember
what he looked like.
All I remember was
his soft, kind voice.

the lake itself from
far away
as if a faint image of the
country roared
like the distant sound
of a loose bull

it had
qualities of the music
I heard
in earlier fears
that so scared and enchanted
me and carried
me across the mysterious
water and dark
pine forests

For the doctor
immediately after
with too much
chatter created
almost the same
symptoms as a
seizure. numb.
Hands dizzy light
feeling ting-ling
static in head
took the medicine
relieved symptoms
disoriented
confused. Poor
circulation
stuffy feeling
in chest
feet strange like I
was going to pass out.

Lonely Face
Set back in the
northwoods.
Island at the site
of a great ancient
fortress
It is near dawn
the ruins left
behind reflect the
crumbling and
abandoned, but how
by a great
majestic, a great
concentration
of strength, valor
fierce and numerous
battles were fought
and in the afternoon
a thin trail
of high concentration
of spirits in a small
micro space.

with all its
flashing lights
and razzle-dazzle
along the commercial
strip could
be found mostly
big-time hustle
oh and then in other
paths of the city
the disco Inferno
a famous gay district.
Beyond the
boundaries
of the lake
an invisible radiation
forces
So powerful and yet
invisible.
The city smoldered
with immeasurable heat
and sizzled out each rampart.
It was a smoldering
of old consciousness
which generated fright.

when I awoke
the first thing that
I heard was a faint
and distant sound,
very far away.
along the lake's
horizon
the mystical melody
came trickling
Entrancing
across the waters
The piper came
calling

incredible heat
incomprehensible
to the common
yet, intensely
supernatural and
a small portion
yet formidable threat
destruction to
the entire world.

The lake itself, shimmering
and reflecting the glimmering
of distant colors
lightly, red, green
neon, fluorescent
blue, shocking pink
fading near far-old
somewhere.
The lake was
conveniently located by
the freeway so one
could park off in the grass
and rest on the bank.
All around the
side were bushes
enclosed in angles
so you could see clearly
the shape of the decks,
silhouetted against
the mooing brush of deep
forest.
Darkness was spooky
and the forest still.

At the lake July 1st.
I found my own
separate corner of
peace and sanity
multi-colored
glittering particles
scattered thru
the placid opaqueness

Like smooth glass
partially illuminated
on the Boon dock
almost glowing

I followed thru the trees
Along the sunny banks
into the
transport place
surrounding shadows
of who knows?

Silent almost
as if waiting
for something
very violent.
Little appeared
from far away
but the distinctive lake.
The tranquility was there.

On the left bank
he and I downed the
bottle of sweet,
country wine, maybe cherry.
The lakeshore seemed peaceful
for away from the remote spot,
lay a hub of activity,
topless bars,
beer hall brawls,
domestic disputes,
beatings, stealing,
hustling massive
evil energy.

Charles decided he wanted
to split again to
outer regions and
other cities
unexplored.
I had to
then get Charles to
the bank and bus station and worry over
how to keep the bit still left
to me before I withdrew it for him
again.
I told him I would split
with him that very
same day after
errands.

I thought living around
the Elderly would
preserve my mental
health and perhaps
give tranquility and
extract rejuvenating
sources to salvage
my mental and
physical state.

Sea of Jordan
salt
so salty
when the sea overflows
it devastates
pours her lava and villages
volcano must cease to erupt
Don't lay dormant
diminish and
go away forever
dilution

Bus Ride to Mid-nite

We oozed along
the neon row

Green, red, and
Blue aglow

we knew the task
was not easy

But the motivation
was strong enough

184

What are we products of?
Middle class boys and girls
who mushroomed
forth in spring from
the suburbs in a terrific boom.
We were not ready
for it. Cut off from
the real world, spoiled,
and with no one to pick up
after us.
This phenomenon is very
common throughout our culture.
But as we grew up those
who chose not to go
to college, took another path.

Rumbling, soaring, hotrods
streaming along the parkways,
all the way up and into white plains
long blonde hairs
shimmering and shaking
to the early autumn flakes
bouncing beside the bumper
kissed with grace
aristocratic poise
long embraced
We held our breath, with each kiss
and played on you
your teddy bear has never seen it
your true bed untouched
baby doll cries before you feed her
she knows not what will come.
nor does the teeny-weeny pink comforter
ever think you'll leave it.
barrettes, still a fascination
stay in my top drawer
my head is their day home, and my hair
a soft place to sleep

We are still inside our house
that lies one side up
covered by brush
the other side juts out over the landscape
we speak in platitudes
until that too is shattered
by a noise outside
outside there in the unknown
we can hardly see it
it is too dark, perhaps the darkest
night of the year
the whiteness of our house
with trimmings of
crystal and jewel are our
only hope and our only refuge
from the darkness
for we are afraid of the darkness
those two out there whoever they are
cannot come inside for they are two
evil musicians two raving minstrels
that terrorize lives like ours

the first thing I saw on
the morning of my Birthday was
that it had snowed.
My father called while I was
finishing my coffee.
He said it was still snowing
when he left the house
earlier that morning.
I am a snow child! I
started crying after I hung
up. Clouds started forming
in my coffee. The mist
became transformed into
a birthday of the past
when I got to eat cake
with a pink frosting.
Crystals formed on
the cake crumbs into
clumps. It was so sweet.

My mother helped me make my bed.
We were going to take a dish of snow
and pour maple syrup over it.

He runs and runs.
Not knowing where he
goes
instinct carries him

thru ditches, across
leveled fields, beneath
bridges, over aqua ducts,
gradually his space
become narrowed
and in ~~special~~ interval perspec
perspective, his choice
is lessened
less alternative ~~beats~~
~~this result in this~~
~~direction be~~ renders
his direction frantic

June 24th

the first thing I saw on the morning of my Birthday that it had snowed. My father called while I was fixing my coffee. He said it was still snowing when he left the house earlier that morning. I am a snow chief! I started crying after I hung up. Clouds started forming in my coffee, the mist became transformed into a beautiful man. I remarked a birthday, of the past when I got to eat cake with frosting. Ice crystals formed on the cake creamers forming stiff little foaming granular lumps, it was

could see my breath.
Huffing and puffing I
carefully rolled the
(newly fallen)
front yard snow into
big balls solid balls
forming "frosty".
As a child, I idolized
frosty the snowman
and when the first
warm days came
he melted away.
Strongly I wished
brew there would be
other frosties?

About the Author

Claire Burch began to put together *Stranger On the Planet—The Small Book of Laurie*, after Laurie, one of her three daughters, died of an overdose of heroin in 1994. The book was a place to put her feelings, which included raw rage at a society that still doesn't do much for people with Laurie's problems beyond giving them psychiatric names and self-fulfilling prophecy phrases like dual diagnosis. She hoped that reading Laurie's own words and seeing her own drawings, might help others to understand what was heartbreaking but sometimes lovable in her grown yet still "wild child," and—because of the book—at least know some of Laurie's thoughts, and that she had existed.

Previous books by Claire Burch are *Stranger in the Family* (Bobbs Merrill), *Notes of a Survivor* (Westbeth Poet's Press), *Careers in Psychiatry* (Macmillan), *Solid Gold Illusion* (Norwood Press), *You Be the Mother Follies, Goodbye My Coney Island Baby,* and *Homeless in the Nineties* (Regent Press). She is also a visual artist and filmaker.

Her writing has appeared in *Life* (Special Report cover story), *Saturday Review, The New Republic, McCalls, Madamoiselle, Redbook, Good Housekeeping, Southwest Review, Arts and Sciences,* and assorted magazines and anthologies.

"People give you a lot of things but they seldom give you something you most want, namely something to stick to the walls of your mind. This you have done for me in your writing. My desk looks like the sweepings of a subway car. I never know when I pick up a piece of paper from it, what world I will be in for the next few minutes. And then I pick up your writing and am completely transported into your world. Your essential gift is that you restore a sense of importance and dignity to personal relationships and personal concerns. I liked what I read and was made easier by it. I thank you for the emotional and spiritual food they have given me."

—Norman Cousins
Saturday Review